THE THINGS KIDS SAY

Ricardo Aranda Falvay

Illustrated by:
José Miguel Martínez Alemán

Published by All Bilingual Press.

Seattle, WA.

All Bilingual Press
www.allbilingual.com

ISBN: 979-8-9897946-5-2

Printed in the USA.

To my children, who always make me love, laugh, and think.

-Ricardo

Para mi mamá. Que su recuerdo viva siempre en los cuentos de mis hijos.

-Ricardo

Our Familia

This collection is a true story, inspired by real events. It captures the memorable moments from the first ten years of our children growing up bilingual.

From the moment they pronounced their first words, I collected their touching, funny, and insightful remarks and shared them on social media for the world to enjoy. Their unfiltered innocence has made us laugh, they've made us think, and often left us speechless.

We've always enjoyed looking back on those early years, and although I'm sure every parent has heard similar comments, many seem quite unique given the bilingual education that happens in our multicultural family.

This book celebrates every child's innocent expression and pays tribute to the beauty of bilingual minds. It encourages us all to look at the world through their eyes.

Everything in this book is presented exactly as it was said.

Ricardo

Ricky
Becky
Papi
Mami
Abuela

NEGOTIATING CON NÚMEROS

Learning languages can often start with numbers, forever changing how kids interact with the world and their parents. With their dual language abilities, bilingual children develop problem-solving skills that improve their chances of winning every conversation.

Me: Becky, ¡voy a empezar a contar!
Becky: One, two, three.

1 year old

Me: Becky, it's time to shower.
Becky: ¡No!
Me: ...Ooooneeeee...
Becky: ...Twoooooo...

2 years old

Me: Vamos, Becky.
Becky: Can you give me five more minutes?
Me: Ok!
Becky: Six! No, no, eight, eight!

4 years old

Me: Cinco minutos más, ¿Ok? ¿Me escucharon?
Becky: ¡Sí! Can you say it again?

4 years old

Me: Rebecca, uno...dos...
Becky: Tres, cuatro, cinco, seis, siete, ocho, nueve, diez.

4 years old

FANTASYLANDIA

A child's imagination can turn the ordinary into extraordinary, and bilingual kids' mental agility and cultural awareness make them exceptionally creative. Their imagination offers fresh perspectives and reminds us that the world is full of fantasy.

Becky: Papi, where are we going?
Me: A la casa, hija.
Becky: But I want to go to Disney World.

2 years old

Becky: Papi, my Moana and you Heihei.

2 years old

Me: Ricky, ¿tú dónde naciste?
Ricky: En Nunca Jamás.

3 years old

Ricky: Papi, yo tengo una idea. Tú puedes ser Batman y podemos salvar el día.

3 years old

Me: Becky, ¿te cepillaste los dientes?
Becky: Papi, I'm a salamander.
Me: ¡Las salamandras también se cepillan los dientes!
Becky: Not in Frozen II.

3 years old

Ricky: Papi, ¿el Salón de la Justicia, queda en Gotham City o Metrópolis?

3 years old

Becky: ...And the stormtroopers lived happily ever after.

4 years old

Becky: Papi, I want to be Peter Pan's daughter.

5 years old

RAISING NIÑOS BILINGÜES

Raising kids creates some of life's most memorable moments, and having bilingual children makes it even more special. Their innocent multilingual remarks and multicultural interests are a testament to their ever-growing minds.

Ricky: Papi dice marrón, Mami dice café, yo digo brown.

3 years old

Becky: Papi, how do you say ok en español?

3 years old

Ricky: Mami, ¿por qué rojo en español tiene más letras que red en inglés?

4 years old

Ricky: Papi, el pollo está muy soft para mi mouth.

4 years old

Becky: Can you buy a pet gallo so it can wake us up?

5 years old

Becky: Papi, now can we wake up? We can go find *leche* and *café*!

6 years old

Becky: Yo quiero un blanket, mis feet están fríos.

7 years old

Ricky: Is *jonrón* supposed to be "home run" in Spanish?

9 years old

Ricky: 12/12 is the last day of the year where no one will ever know if you wrote it the Spanish way or the English way.

9 years old

Ricky: Papi, it's strange. Say thank you and goodbye in Spanish!
Me: Thank you es "*gracias*" y bye es "*adiós*."
Ricky: See? ¡Gracias a Dios!

9 years old

SMALL COMEDIANTES

A child's humor is the most spontaneous and genuine kind. With their innocent perspectives, unfiltered comments, or a playful blend of reality and fantasy, bilingual kids can always make us laugh even at the simplest things.

Becky: I don't like Lunes!

3 years old

Ricky: Papi, ¿en qué planeta vive la abuela?

3 years old

Becky: Mmm bacon! I never thought I would eat this good!

4 years old

Me: Ricky, ¿cuándo te pusiste tan pesado?
Ricky: Es porque he estado comiendo rocas.

4 years old

Becky: Papi, are you thinking what I'm thinking?
Me: Probably not; what are you thinking?
Becky: Let's make a time machine!

4 years old

Me: Ricky, si tú tienes 5 años ¿Por qué tus medias dicen "2-3 Years"?
Ricky: Porque two and three is five.

5 years old

Ricky: Papi, mi mano no tiene pila así que voy a llamar con mi pie.

5 years old

Ricky: Papi, I want to look in your brain to see what's going on.

6 years old

UNEXPECTED COMENTARIOS

Kids sometimes say the most unexpected things, and when they're bilingual, it adds a delightful twist to any conversation. Their broader vocabulary can spark creativity and lead to new and surprising comments.

Becky: Papi, I have a problem; why can't I see my own eyes?

3 years old

Ricky: Papi, ¿tú puedes alcanzar el sol?

4 years old

Becky: Papi, don't walk and sing at the same time, you might fall.

4 years old

Ricky: Papi, cuando está lloviendo no sirve mi x-ray vision.

4 years old

Me: I'm going to have to call the Apple Store.
Becky: Can you buy some applesauce?

4 years old

Ricky: Papi, hoy hicimos mean people drill en la escuela. Es como hide
     and seek.

5 years old

Becky: Papi, can I have my own credit card?

5 years old

Me: Hijo, ¡no te arranques el diente!
Ricky: But I want to get money!

6 years old

Becky: Papi, are you going to work out until you look like Captain America?

6 years old

Ricky: Papi, when I'm big, I hope they invent teleportation technology.

8 years old

BETWEEN HERMANOS

Growing up with a bilingual brother or sister offers a natural immersion in language and creates a bond that lasts a lifetime. Bilingual siblings provide support and encouragement while creating a place to learn and celebrate their multicultural upbringing.

Becky: Ricky, you're my big brother, so can you go get me leche?

3 years old

Ricky: Becky, Santa Claus is watching you!

5 years old

Ricky: Becky, tomorrow, do you want to go back in time?

6 years old

Ricky: Becky, did you do something nice today?
Becky: Yes, I let Papi take my iPad away.

6 and 3 years old

Ricky: Becky, what are you waiting for?
Becky: For my birthday!

7 and 3 years old

Ricky: Becky, is it ok if I call you Thing 2?

7 years old

Me: Becky, tú eres muy cómica.
Ricky: Yes, that you got from Papi's side of the family.

8 years old

Ricky: Becky, I'm going to teach you about misunderstood animals.

9 years old

WOMEN AL PODER

Moms coach their children by leading by example. Bilingual moms often balance the demands of career, family, and personal aspirations with creating an inclusive and culturally rich environment for their children to grow in. They become the role models of the next generation of strong and confident children.

Becky: Papi, I'm not a baby anymore. I'm a big girl now.

Ricky: Mami, hay que poner reglas en esta casa.

Becky: Papi, does the mom have more responsibilities than the dad?

Ricky: Mami, ¿dónde está papi?
Mami: Ya se fue al trabajo, Ricky.
Ricky: ¿Y entonces quien te va a hacer tu café?

2 years old

3 years old

5 years old

Becky: You make the rules for now since Mami is not here!

Becky: Papi, who is your favorite girl in the world?
Me: You!
Becky: Shouldn't it be Mami?

Ricky: Papi, tomorrow I'm going to call Mami to come back.

Me: ¡Becky, mañana vas a la escuela todo el día!
Becky: Are you telling me or asking me?

Becky: It would be really cool if the next president is a woman.

BIG PERSONALIDADES

Children are great at sharing their points of view and voicing their opinions, even at an early age. Bilingual ones often show strong social skills and increased confidence, which helps with their strong presence and offers a small glimpse into their developing personalities.

Me: Becky, ya es hora de ir a la escuela.
Becky: No! Becky go night night.

2 years old

Me: ¿Qué quieres desayunar Ricky?
Ricky: ¡Pasta!
Me: Pasta no es para el desayuno.
Ricky: Why?

2 years old

Becky: Papi, I'm keeping my eyes on you.

4 years old

Mami: Ricky, baja por favor.
Ricky: No gracias, Mami, estoy bostezando.

4 years old

Becky: Papi, if you say no, I will puppy eye you.

4 years old

Me: Ricky, ya hay que arreglarnos.
Ricky: No, ¡yo ya me veo guapo!

4 years old

BEDTIME CUENTOS

A kid's world is full of excitement, which makes it hard for them to sleep. Parents, on the other hand, spend years of sleepless nights caring for them and making sure they get much needed rest to develop the mental and social benefits that come from growing up bilingual.

Ricky: Papi, dormir es la cosa más aburrida del mundo.

4 years old

Becky: Papi, I don't like sleeping. It's boring. It's just lay, close your eyes. Done.

4 years old

Becky: It's morning, Papi. You can stop sleeping now.

4 years old

Me: Ricky, es hora de despertarse.
Ricky: Después de que vea comiquitas en mi cabeza.

4 years old

Becky: Papi, when will you stop sleeping in so much?

6 years old

Me: ¡Los días que se paran temprano, se duermen temprano!
Ricky: Eh! No! I have no idea who told you that!

7 years old

Me: Ricky, mañana hay que pararse antes que Mami.
Ricky: Yeah, that's easy to do!

7 years old

Ricky: It's lazy day Papi, relax!

7 years old

WORKING PADRE

Balancing work and family life can be challenging. Thankfully, bilingual kids turn out to be great helpers for their working parents. Their problem-solving skills, adaptability, and broad understanding of the world provide a unique perspective on everything we do and help us manage it all.

Becky: Papi, today are you going to trabajar en el medio de la noche otra vez?

3 years old

Becky: Papi, I'm going to work with you because you need help!

3 years old

Ricky: Papi, are you tired of me and Becky disobeying the rules?

6 years old

Ricky: Papi, do you have time for a family meeting right now?

6 years old

Becky: Papi, can I get vacaciones también?

6 years old

Ricky: Papi, how hard is it to be a father?

7 years old

Ricky: Papi, can I give you a parent's quiz?

7 years old

Ricky: Papi, right now, are you grumpy Papi or happy Papi?

8 years old

Ricky: Papi, want feedback?

9 years old

THE JOYS OF SER PADRE

Being a father of bilingual kids comes with amazing rewards. It offers the opportunity to celebrate life's achievements, but also to take a critical look at your life through their eyes. All these moments, filled with learning, laughter, and love, make parenting a joyful and insightful experience.

Becky: Papi, one day you should really wear a tutu!

4 years old

Becky: Papi, one day you should really paint your nails.

4 years old

Becky: Papi, I think you need more medicine now.
Me: Sí, puede ser que me tome algo ahorita.
Becky: Which one do you want? Cherry? Or grape?

5 years old

Becky: Papi, you are a great cook. You should work at Domino's.

5 years old

Becky: Papi, tomorrow, for Father's Day, we're going to have a nail salon.

5 years old

Becky: I like snuggling with you 'cause you're the warmest in the family.

5 years old

Ricky: Papi, if I had to sell you, you would be so expensive!

8 years old

Ricky: Papi, when you were a kid, were you like me?
Me: Igualito.
Becky: And like me?
Me: También.

9 and 5 years old

BUILDING MEJORES PERSONAS

Bilingual kids grow up embracing kindness and responsibility. Navigating diverse languages and cultures helps them understand, appreciate, and respect their surroundings. It creates empathy and motivates them to make the world a better place.

Ricky: Papi, ¿por qué no le decimos gracias a Alexa?

4 years old

Becky: It's ok, Papi, never give up!

4 years old

Becky: Papi, we have to take care of Earth; it's the only planet we have.

4 years old

Ricky: Papi, are you proud of me?

6 years old

Becky: Papi, can you put me in the best high school and college in the world?

6 years old

Ricky: Papi, what are you going to be when you grow up!?

6 years old

Ricky: Hope helps you get what you want!

8 years old

Ricky: Papi, I'm very lucky to have this type of family.

8 years old

Ricky: Papi, you were right; believing in yourself actually helps.

8 years old

INQUIRING MENTES

Bilingual kids are always curious and eager to explore language and culture, but it doesn't end there. They are driven to ask the most challenging questions and to look for answers to life's mysteries. As they grow, their questions get harder, showing how fascinating their developing little brains work.

Becky: Papi, can you tell me a story inside your mind?

5 years old

Becky: Papi, where did the first dinosaur come from?

6 years old

Becky: Papi, how do they make white chocolate if chocolate is brown?

6 years old

Ricky: Papi, how did it all start?

7 years old

Ricky: Papi, why does time go so fast?

7 years old

Ricky: Papi, what would you do if you were the president?

7 years old

Ricky: Papi, if the H is silent, why even have an H?

8 years old

Ricky: Wouldn't we all be Africans because life started in Africa?

9 years old

Ricky: Papi, tell me the important things in life.

9 years old

Ricky: If you had the chance to time travel, what would you do?

9 years old

A MULTICULTURAL CUENTO DE AMOR

With age comes a more personal curiosity, particularly about love, relationships, and intimate family talks. Bilingual children want to know about their past, how their parents met, and the stories that celebrate their unique diversity and multicultural heritage.

Ricky: Papi, ¿por qué Mami y tu crecieron más rápido que yo?

4 years old

Becky: Mami, did you know every single thing starts as a baby?

5 years old

Ricky: Papi, when and where was the first time you kissed Mami?

6 years old

Becky: Papi, how do kids get saliva and things from their dad if they are born from their mom?

6 years old

Becky: Papi, which of my feet was born first?

7 years old

Ricky: Papi, do you and Mami have like an eye language?
Me: Why do you ask?
Ricky: Mami is always looking at you.

9 years old

Becky: Ricky, do you remember being born? What did you see?
Ricky: A doctor!

7 & 10 years old

GETTING OLD ES UN REGALO

Aging gracefully is accepting that life is a fabulous journey. However, children have a way of pointing out the less attractive side of getting old. With their innocent observations, bilingual kids remind us to embrace the beauty of growing older.

Ricky: Papi, ¿todavía te falta para tener tus 100 años?

4 years old

Ricky: Papi, ¿por qué hay gente que no tiene pelo?

4 years old

Ricky: Papi, ¿sabes por qué siempre te digo cosas? Porque siempre te olvidas cosas.

4 years old

Me: Becky, tienes mucho pelo.
Becky: Y tú no tienes mucho pelo.

5 years old

Becky: Papi, did you know every step you get older, you get kinder?

5 years old

Becky: My padrino y tú might be bald buddies.

5 years old

Ricky: Papi, remember, you're a thousand years older than I am.

6 years old

Ricky: Your hair is really white.
Me: Eso se llama canas.
Ricky: Some sort of sickness?

10 years old

Ricky: Papi, when you die, can I have your phone?

SOWING NUEVAS RAICES

The children of emigrants embody a new blend of cultures, bridging their parent's heritage with their newfound home. Bilingual kids get to create their own identities with their exposure to foods, words, and customs. Put simply, bilingual children embody the spirit of new multicultural families.

Becky: Papi, can you show me how to do Arepas?

3 years old

Becky: Papi, it smells like tequeño.

4 years old

Ricky: Papi, ¿toda tu familia es de Venezuela?
Me: Sí, hijo.
Ricky: ¿Y todos se fueron a vivir a otro lado como tú?

5 years old

Becky: Papi, I made a decision of where I'm going to live when I grow up
Me: ¿Dónde?
Becky: Venezuela.

5 years old

Ricky: ¿Qué es una vaca mariposa? Does it have wings?
Becky: I thought it had butterfly wings.

6 years old

Me: ¿Dónde quedaron mis cholas?
Ricky: I don't know what "cholas" means, so I don't know.

7 years old

Me: Becky, ¡Ricky tiene dinero del Ratoncito Pérez!
Ricky: Papi, it's called the tooth fairy, not a rat!

6 years old

About the Author:

Ricardo is a world traveler who carries Venezuela in his heart. A devoted father of two, he and his Ecuadorian wife cherish the richness of their multicultural and bilingual family life. Ricardo is a passionate global marketer, educated at Cornell University, who recently discovered a newfound love for telling his family stories.

Follow their stories at:

@growingup.bilingue

About the Illustrator:

José is a Venezuelan artist and software engineer who creates illustrations for storybooks, comics, and video games. His art draws from various influences, from Western comic books to classic Japanese animated films. Always eager to grow his skills, José loves diving into Latin American stories, experimenting with new styles, and getting lost in video games.

Follow his work at:

@fkaexe